"Stephen Lightbown's poetry challe[nges] us, as we follow him from life-threa[t] after injury, with everything that inv[...] and intimate collection, offering g[...] frustration, hope and humour of an i[ndividual] journey towards acceptance and rehabilitation."
Owen Lowery

"Thanks to Stephen Lightbown's first book of poems we get to see through the eyes of a wheelchair user. Where a beach can be 'a war, a match raging between ears', where 'seats can applaud' in football stadiums, where your own wheelchair can be a person waiting for you to wake up. Almost anything in Stephen's poems has the potential to walk. These are straight-talking autobiographical poems which are traumatic, celebratory, humorous and always more than one thing. That is what I know about living with a disability: we have to write our narratives, because the ones written about us, the ones that reduce us to benefit scroungers or pitiful charity cases, speak against our complex humanity, and Stephen, with every poem he writes, gives us an honest glimpse into his."
Raymond Antrobus

"Stephen Lightbown's debut collection Only Air *is deeply moving and at times wryly funny. His life-changing accident is the lens through which family, friendships and love are explored, bringing them into sharp and poignant focus. Beyond the intimate circle of personal relationships, the poems reveal a world where expedience and ignorance can create a hostile environment for a wheelchair user. Poems harness a variety of registers from low-key understatement in 'Independent Train Travel', which sees a passenger treated as luggage, to the wonderful imaginative leap and surreal tone of 'Bear Off a Leash', which personifies the poet's ready-to-rear rage on a busy street. Stephen has transformed his experiences into remarkable poetry that gives insight, pleasure and huge enjoyment."*
Lisa Kelly

Stephen is a poet and disability rights champion. He was born in Blackburn, Lancashire. In 1996, aged 16, he experienced a life-changing accident whilst sledging in the snow and is now paralysed from below the waist. In 2016, twenty years after the accident, Stephen started writing poetry about his life as a wheelchair user. When not writing and performing poetry he spends his days working for the NHS. Stephen now lives in Bristol and has a long-held ambition to read his poems in his Northern accent in New York. *Only Air* is Stephen's first full length poetry collection.

www.stephenlightbown.com   @spokeandpencil

Only Air

Stephen Lightbown

Burning Eye

BurningEyeBooks
Never Knowingly
Mainstream

Copyright © 2019 Stephen Lightbown

The author asserts the moral right under the Copyright, Designs and Patents Act 1988 to be identified as the author of this work.

This edition published by Burning Eye Books 2019

www.burningeye.co.uk

@burningeyebooks

Burning Eye Books
15 West Hill, Portishead, BS20 6LG

ISBN 978-1-911570-59-2

Only Air

To Jim,
my first &
still my main
hero. J Thanks
for being a
legend. Stephen. oc

CONTENTS

ACCIDENT
  This So-Called Life: Part Two   10
  Trials and Tribulations   12
  Mark's Story, 1996   13
  Pier Review   14
  Grandad's Greenhouse   15
  Big Feet, No Space   17
  A Paralympic Dream Stuck in 2012   18

STABILISING
  For Graham, the Hairdresser   20
  Join the Dots   22
  Should Have Kept Quiet   23
  Five   26
  Three Little Birds   27
  Independent Train Travel   28
  The Wisdom of Mum   29

SITTING UP
  The Arranged Marriage   32
  XL   33
  The Woe of Toe   34
  Bear Off a Leash   35
  A Fiver, an Injured Gazelle, and You – a Tiger   37
  Wheelchair: Lighthouse of the Streets   38
  Only Desert Remains   39

STARTING AGAIN
30,000ft   42
The Barbados Wave   43
Finding Myself in NYC   45
The Great Wall of China   46
Before Time   47
First Kiss   48
Tell Me What You Know Through Tarot   49

SETBACKS
The Three Stages of Aging   52
Climbing the Ladder   53
Under Appeal   55
This Is How It Feels to Be...   56
The Race   57
Garlic Boy   60
Walking Again Through Avatar   61

GOING HOME
Unwelcome Home   64
On The Number 76 in Bristol   65
Seeing Me Again   66
Love in an IKEA Blue Bag   67
Scratchcard Memories of Dad   68
Weller's Wood   69
White   70

ACCIDENT

Judge, jury, executioner. The surgeon speaks a short sentence that starts a life stretch. 'You'll never walk again.'

THIS SO-CALLED LIFE: PART TWO

1.
God didn't come for me that day.
I remember the exact moment my eyes opened
and I looked skywards. All I saw was blue.
No clouds, no sun, no help.
It was the aftermath of my accident
when the life I had carelessly called mine fought
to stay or leave. I didn't believe this was real.
In amongst the stillness and distant sirens,
I sought answers. I questioned if He would come.

2.
I'm drowning internally, lungs heavy with death.
I press the button that feeds morphine and there's
emptiness. Am I ready to say goodbye?
Mum sits by the side of my hospital bed.
She hasn't moved in a week.
Her red jumper the only thing I recognise.
I look into her eyes, fatigued with pain. Anguish etched
where only days before I saw laughter.
I go on for her.

3.
I can no longer meet my actual maker.
Forget a stairway to heaven; in my wheelchair
I can't even navigate the steps into Dad's new home.
Saturday nights of spag bol with a round of bread.
Soundtracked by his familiar laugh, wheeze, cough
to *Noel's House Party*; a regular fixture of my childhood
since he left with his keys on the table. Dad believed
it was the right thing to do. It wasn't. Now all I have
are phone calls, where silence speaks of regret.

4.
I'm nineteen, it's three years to the day after my accident.
The England football manager has been sacked
for his belief that people born with a disability
pay for sins made in a previous existence.
Public outcry reincarnated into PR disaster.
Now he collects his P45 as I collect my benefits.
I wonder what mistake karma wants to correct with me;
am I being punished for actions taken in my first sixteen years?
Will I ever know why fate chose me?

5.
I'm sat outside Dad's house. I'm twenty-one.
But I don't want the keys to the door
he is forever still behind. Today is the day of his funeral.
My younger brother is with me. Neither of us say a word.
For most of my life Dad was absent; now he is gone.
I know he loved us, that he wished time had turned
out differently. I want to tell him we can't choose the path
we take, but we can control the way we walk it. I miss him.
And yet, for one last time, I believe he is here.

6.
Years later a man approaches me on Tottenham Court Road
and clutches an old black Bible to his heart.
He holds the book in one hand as though the source
by which he breathes, and softly places his other
on my shoulder. The man tells me we are all God's children,
and that He forgives me, He can make me walk again.
All I have to do is believe. But how can I?
When I don't know why He took my legs
and then Dad, before I was ready to say goodbye to either.

TRIALS AND TRIBULATIONS

From toddler to teen
I was as excitable as a Labrador puppy.
I'd bump from one accident to the next.
The first-aid box and a mischievous
grin were never far away.

Spent more time in A&E than after-school clubs,
collected scars in the way friends traded
Panini stickers and shinies.
Told myself I was indestructible.

I believed that to be true until a rancorous winter
arrived like a mugging in the night.
I would change forever.
Couldn't swap this sticker.

*

As my frozen clothes – jacket, hoodie, jumper, T-shirt,
jeans, boxers, socks x 2, trainers, shield of invincibility –
are surgically removed, I think back
to the messages I chose to ignore from the
stitches, bruises and plaster casts I've worn before.
Finally, it becomes clear.
I understand the shadow in the room.
It is danger.
It is real.
It is here.
It has come for me.

MARK'S STORY, 1996

The common room. That's where I spend my free time. They are not wrong, mate. In here we have the same thing in common: a sense of trying to figure out what has happened. Can't leave, got rooms we share with strangers, lights out at ten, queue for the payphone. The name says *hospital* but it's a prison with a stethoscope. I certainly don't deserve to get sent down because I failed to surf a flight of stairs in my gaff in Salford. Visiting times can do one. Families shuffle in with smuggled contraband. And we are back to that room. Snooker table, vending machine, too many tears. Then there's the other tables. Laid out like a Strangeways visiting room, only on one side the fuzz have those plastic chairs; on the other, just a space reserved for us inmates and our prison-issue chariots. All trying to figure out the crimes we committed to be given a life stretch. Prisoners in our own legs, I reckon. Still, at least they let us smoke. I used to be sound with my hands, was a mechanic and a top one at that. Nothing I couldn't fettle. Now I have to tape a cigarette to my wrist. Fingers as useful as a spanner sat in the toolbox in my locked-up garage. That was my first task. Before I started thinking about leaving here and conquering Kilimanjaro I wanted to at least hold a fag to my mouth. I know I shouldn't, but who knows what is and isn't going to do you in? I used to be able to master any machine. Cars, bikes, even the odd sixteen-wheeler. Anything with a set of seats and an engine. But this chair, man. Turn it in. This is a different fucking rodeo. More beast than transport. Got a mind of its own and just getting out of bed takes the effort of running a marathon. Can I even say that anymore? What do I do now, roll a marathon? Chance would be a fine thing. Chance is what put me here. No thanks, can't be mithered. I'm just gaggin' for someone to tell me straight. Every word is said with a tattooed smile. Like each sentence is a frosted bun straight off the counter at the local butty shop. That every Wednesday when I'm meant to be at five-a-side my boots will never leave my sports bag. That I'll be one of 40,000 people with a spinal cord injury, more or less the same that can fit in Maine Road. Just tell us that the road ahead is gonna be full of cobbles. And I will feel anything but common.

13

PIER REVIEW

Weston-super-Mare arcades in November. Slot machines,
mountains of soft toys, candyfloss tumbleweed,
hibernating donkeys, ruined sandcastles, tide out till June.
Children lost in duffel coats. Me coins in hand ready to win.

I'd already won your heart, now I was going
to bag you a bear the size of Belgium. Ball, hoop,
put ball through hoop. Repeat. Claim my prize and prove
my life partner potential. Simple. Indifferent and woozy
on vinegar, you set about your fish and chips.

All the fun at the fair became white noise. I was at one
with the ball until, like Jaws nibbling
on an inflatable banana, disaster. I let go and watched
the ball change course as though guided
by a malevolent navigation system. It landed flush
on your Friday night supper. I'd had a
Weston-super-nightmare.

I looked at the battered sea dweller and sad spuds
forlorn on the floor. I looked at the ball now rolling
seductively between your feet and my wheels.
And then unfathomably returned to the game.
With one chip left bereft on a plastic blue fork,
you now looked at me.

I didn't need a seaside fortune teller
to tell me this game was over.

GRANDAD'S GREENHOUSE

Mowed short at the back and sides
and longer down the middle,
we stood on a lawn manicured
by memories of the military.

Everything here had its place.
The bird table where marigold hands
placed crumbs at Christmas.
The tree stump and flower beds,
the lean-to garage and various sheds.

And Grandad's greenhouse.
Complete with one pane of glass
on which he'd hand-engraved a braying
horse. Hung like a Renaissance masterpiece
on a see-through wall.

Two years, six inches and three
shoe sizes was all that separated us.
Our combined age wouldn't
yet make a single teenager.

We didn't need to be told the garden
was not for playing, but still we silently
kicked the football from one
accomplice to the other.

Catastrophe came with a misplaced pass.
Shattering the stencilled equine.
Raining shards into tomorrow's salad.

Fear forced roots to spring
from our careless feet,
trees now bound to the ground
with remorse.

Four heavy eyelids fell like
the last leaves of autumn.
When we blinked, too shocked
and too soon for tears,
we saw Grandad.

It was not anger I recall
but out-of-place calmness.
A gentle look
that said we would not be felled
but instead allowed to grow.

Rage is never the answer.
Not all lessons are taught in school.

*

I lay in traction on the Spinal Unit
holding a letter as beautifully arranged
as the garden in which I once stood.
Each word formed from his elegant handwriting
and placed with as much precision
as his Lancashire red rosebushes.

Your mother is worried,
she tells me you are as thin as the canes
I use to hold up the tomatoes.
You need to eat. I'll send vegetables.
Keep your strength up.

*

He wrote to me every week I was in hospital.
I didn't miss a meal again.
Six months it took me to reach home.

The garden,
the greenhouse,
Grandad.

Now everything is gone
apart from a shoebox full of letters.

BIG FEET, NO SPACE

This is a message to tiny places
and dainty spaces.
I'm a six-foot-seven-inches-tall wheelchair user.
That means I have a lot of leg
and plenty of feet.

Feet that stick out and can clear
a low shelf when trying
to do a manoeuvre
in a supermarket aisle.

Like a double-decker bus doing
a three-point turn in a skip,
the BFG using a teabag
as a trampoline,
a bear skating the Bolero
on an ice cube
or a couple dancing a foxtrot
on a postage stamp.

What I'm trying to say
is that me and small areas
just don't get along.
I think it's time we took a break.
I just need some

space.

A PARALYMPIC DREAM STUCK IN 2012

A golden mustard globule falls like a medal from the sky.
It lands, unseen, in a family-sized Diet Coke for one.
He shoots, he scores. I watch intently as a hot dog hand
is clapped against a Team GB foam finger.
A capacity crowd, wheelchair basketball at the O2.
The unthinkable happening.

I count how long the adulation will last. Two thousand,
four hundred seconds. Four ten-minute quarters of fitting in.
My height, now useless at slam dunks, but once good at the game
we watch, grasps at the hysteria in hungry swipes.
I turn to my wife. *Where were all these people yesterday?*
She replies, *Just enjoy the fact that they are here.*

Tomorrow this city will return to the home of good intentions,
empty promises and inaccessible tube stations.
Cheers for chairs will be as distant as the shrill full-time whistle
soon to be blown. In the morning I will play a new game.
Reflection roulette. Which version of me will London see
tomorrow? Will this Paralympic legacy make it to Monday?

After the match I tweet the star player for Team GB, *Hey Dan,
don't know if you remember me, we played together 10 years ago.
Watched you at the O2 tonight. Thought you were brill.* A tiny bird
brings a message. *Hey man, course I remember you. How are things?*

I'm not sure, I think. *Gr8*, I reply.

STABILISING

A plaster won't heal a punctured lung, pain is not caused by the air we breathe. You can't suffocate on fear.

FOR GRAHAM, THE HAIRDRESSER

We were strangers yesterday.
You were celebrating the interview of a lifetime.
I was tree-bound, backwards on a sledge.

You never did start that job
and I was six months late for dinner.
Now, two accidents later,
we are side by side.
The Spinal Unit emergency zone.
Hospital beds,
IV drips,
shell-shocked families.

Today we fight a battle
against our own bad luck.
Both of us pointlessly debating decisions
that led us here rather than home.

Sleep punctuated by things
that go beep in the night.
Morning handovers
and the next dose of bad news.
Fearful of being sent home.
Waiting for wounds to heal
that may always stay raw.

Tomorrow we start again.
Our families will help us rebuild.
We will remain neighbours for half a year.
You, my elder mentor, and me,
desperate for your wisdom despite the fact
we are as new to this as each other.

Your fingers will no longer grip.
But you will grasp the severity of our predicament.
And your lips will still move freely
as you talk in your Liverpool lilt about what you have lost:

the career as a hairdresser; the movement
in your hands.

Months later we will be discharged,
and we will never see each other again.

JOIN THE DOTS

The sign on the door says *Intensive Care*.
Crisp hospital sheets on top of me.
Fear keeps me still.
Traction keeps me stable. Time is delayed.

My eyes fix straight up,
lost in tiny holes in the ceiling tiles.
My own galaxy of stars. A new universe.
My library, my cinema.

A distraction from the horror
around me.
From the groans and despair
of neighbours I can't see.

I lose myself in the ceiling,
the only way to get through the day.
My means of escape.
The dots I am yet to join.

SHOULD HAVE KEPT QUIET

We sit in a Shoreditch café. Breakfast ordered. Haloumi
on a round of hipster beards. You ask me if I've ever felt
like this before. I say yes, *with Alan Shearer.*
Before shared crisps with Lineker.
Before he was a magpie, who shunned silver for adulation,
he was my god in blue and white halves with a rose
on his chest. He was Blackburn Rovers' number 9.

He would rampage on the turf, ball as an extra limb,
eyes forward, power as beauty. Smash balls past ghost
gloved hands, wheel away to the corner flag, one arm
raised in celebration. Classic Alan. I'd stand with my
30,000 strong congregation, our rise and fall an ecstatic
breath from which we exhaled as one,
Shearer Shearer Shearer.

Ewood Park, Blackburn End, row 5, seat 138.
My seat. Where I fell for Alan. Loved him like
a six-week-old puppy loves its owner. Throw me a ball, Alan;
tickle me, Alan; here are your boots, Alan, delivered
with a dog-slobber tongue. So many had worn his number,
but I sang his name like no other. Love? More like life.
Even the seats applauded as we left.

I had Alan's name tattooed on the back of my shirt;
posters of Alan covered my wall like gift wrap.
Alan argues with the referee. Alan wins a header. Alan scores.
Alan in the home kit. Alan in the away kit. Alan in a 1990s
shell-suit not allowed near a naked flame. Alan everywhere.
Wall-to-wall Alan. And one poster of Pamela Anderson,
lifeguard in red, cheek to cheek.

I was twelve when Alan signed for Blackburn.
£3.6 million, a world transfer record in 1992. That's a can of Lilt,
Gregg's pasty and change for a *Beano* in early nineties currency
3.6 million times over. He stayed for four years, scored 130 goals.
That's 130 times he made me jump and grab

for clouds. In 1995 Alan led us to the Premier League title.
Blackburn Rovers English champions. Greatest time of my life.

That was until 27 January 1996 when it snowed.
Great white Tippex start-afresh snow. No football. Anywhere.
So I went sledging instead. I hit a tree.
I broke my back.
Wheelchair user.
Simple as that.
No more feet on terraces.

One week later 30,419 watched Alan score a hat-trick
in a 3-1 victory over our local rivals Bolton Wanderers.
It should have been 30,420.
Mum fed me the score in my hospital bed.
She had covered walls with my posters from home, as though
bandages to heal reality, to give me inspiration. It didn't work.
I needed more than posters. I needed Alan.

I was in intensive care, in formation with seven
other broken teammates thrown together yesterday.
Eyes fixed on the door, thoughts of my own fulltime
for company. In walked Tim Flowers, Blackburn's goalkeeper,
England's number one. Followed by Mike Newell,
one of Alan's fellow forwards.
Then.

Alan.
Fucking.
Shearer.

The heart monitor I was hooked up to
exploded into life, fuelled by embers of mine. Alan
was bundled to one side as nurses rushed to halt
my cardiac arrest that wasn't.
After all these years I had told Alan, through the medium of a heart
monitor, how much I loved him.

In return he gave me a signed copy of his book.
Alan Shearer's Diary of a Season.
It was quite the read.

I realise the halloumi squeak has fallen silent.
I'm back in Shoreditch. I look at you, my new strike partner,
and your dating profile flashes before my eyes. *I like fitness,*
but hate sport, especially football.
I take my cue from the cheese, swallow words with a gulp of tea.
In hindsight I should just have said,
No, dear, I've not felt like this before.

FIVE

I am the middle of Dad's five children.
A brown-haired, green-eyed bullseye
in a swirl of strawberry tops
and blue-tinted observers.
The only one who looks like Mum.
The only one who rolls to attention.
The only one he would send to the posh
neighbour, with the chocolate-brown
creosote fence and the dish on the roof, to collect
old black VHS videotapes at final whistle.
All because Dad didn't want to pay for the privilege.
And yet, for all his flaws, it still takes the five of us
to add up to the sum of Dad.

THREE LITTLE BIRDS

Hey, three little birds,
tattooed on the feet that sleep
next to mine.
What song do you sing?

When you migrate
under the duvet,
in the dying embers of the night.
What song do you sing?

When you build a nest
in the hard dry skin
on the sole of my foot.
Caught in perpetual flight,
with your indelible wings.
What song do you sing?

Each night
you make the long journey
from your side of the bed
to mine.
Whatever the song,
the feel of you
makes my toes dance.

I carry my feet
like disconnected shackles,
so, unaware, I hibernate
until your voice fills my ear
with warmth
as you describe the sensation
of our feet nesting.

INDEPENDENT TRAIN TRAVEL

Behind the suitcases and holdalls the sign reads
PLEASE LEAVE THIS SPACE FREE FOR WHEELCHAIRS.
I boarded the train at Bristol as a passenger, not
a weekend wardrobe. But now at Cardiff I sit amongst
backpacks and baggage, folded-up bikes, pushchairs
and carrier bags digesting ready-made meals. Apparently
invisible. I've been put in my place in front of the ignored
instruction, hidden from embarrassed eyes that won't meet mine.
Put in my place, dignity flushed onto the tracks, away from
the selection of hot and cold snacks. But I am not luggage;
I am a passenger too.

THE WISDOM OF MUM

After the accident
Mum said two words.
Two words that put me
on the path to here.

I remember looking at her,
searching for answers.
In the way a toddler
grills parents from the back seat.

Her response was all I needed.
More wisdom than any lesson I'd sat in,
motivational speech heard, or clinical
pep talk given since the unlucky break.

Nothing changes.

SITTING UP

A wheelchair waits by the side of a bed. It checks its watch. 'He should be up by now,' it thinks.

THE ARRANGED MARRIAGE

The first time we met I didn't want you.
I wasn't ready to acknowledge your existence.

I had no choice but to take you and I resented you for that.
You were confident, brash, all that I wasn't.

But in your own way you needed me.
There were others in line, ready for you.

Yet you and I, we were brought together.
We had to make it work.

The first time was awkward.
I didn't know where to put my hands.

Fumbled across the room.
You were patient; you made me take it gently.

And the first time we went out, it was awful.
I cried, until my head throbbed with fatigue.

I felt everyone stare, judge us.
You didn't care.

You waited, patiently, till I was ready.
And we haven't looked back.

Twenty years together.
Man and chair.

XL

His hugs came
like his T-shirts,
in double XL.
Small ones before bedtime,
safe ones after nightmares,
suffocating ones when he left us.

Months before, pre-hospital visits
and false promises,
I'd told him I no longer
wanted to embrace when
we said goodbye.

Now, I sit up to him, wheels
against his thighs,
back at my eight-year-old
kitchen doorframe notch.

I remember that as the perfect
height to rest my head against
the warm pillow of my father's stomach,
whilst he clamped me reassuringly
into his Benson & Hedges scent.

I ask again, to hold me once more,
so I can feel him squeeze me
back into the safety of my
childhood.

THE WOE OF TOE

Nothing can prepare you
for the first time
your toenail falls off
and you feel no pain,
not even a mild itch.
That is, apart from the
phantom one in your head.

And then your toe wriggles,
like it's free and happy again.
As if an overexcited toddler
released from reins for the first time.
But you didn't ask it to move;
it just did.
Your own toe with a mind of its own.
As though it's a pinkie with a brain.

And then you sit,
wide-eyed, open-mouthed.
Unable to believe.

BEAR OFF A LEASH

I'm out with Bear on Victoria Street.
He pads on all fours beside my wheelchair.
Slaloms his way through soil rain
that falls from freshly watered hanging baskets
perched like floral eagles on London's lampposts.
Metal cranes observe from above as they deliver
skips to third floors of empty shell buildings
not yet with lifts and walls.
Wet nose to the ground, tension
stretches his sinews. His fur bristles.
Moments from mayhem. The street is a treadmill in reverse,
every third door a Pret. Repetition everywhere.
Step step Pret.
Step step Pret.
Step step Pret.
Tourists and commuters momentarily forget their handhelds.
We don't belong here.
I am wary of Bear.
I want to get to the station without incident.
No bag dropped and a thousand hands to help.
No raised kerbs and falling out of my chair.
No collisions with the oblivious and distracted.
A wheelie suitcase here. Double pram there.
Sideways glances. Unseen wrath from Bear.
Bubbles of rage fight for release.
Bear explodes. Chaos.
Now upright he claws at a man on a Boris bike.
Interloper on the pavement,
briefcase and *Metro* in his basket.
He is too close to our tension.
Bear scratches at the fact we are different.
That in this city of a million faces we stand out below eye level.
The commuter cyclist is collateral damage from our rage.
An accident.
Like we once were.
Lava eyes ignore sense. Bear is too strong for me.
I grasp at the space where moments ago he was.

Bear, stop, what are you doing? Let it go, I plead.
Bear replies, *Say he deserved it.*
Bear is AWOL in the woods. Redwoods loom,
their branches retreat.
You're pathetic, forget the chair, stand up for yourself.
Say I was right.
Bear is a dot. Lost to me.
No good ever comes when he is like this.
I know what Bear thinks.
If people want to stare, give them a show.
Take me out from the trees, put me in a big top.
Silence and shame will deliver us to the station.
Bear is right.
Bear is shaking. Furious.

A FIVER, AN INJURED GAZELLE, AND YOU – A TIGER

A cast of two, a one-day-only production. Performed
in the bright lights of London's Piccadilly. The play starts,
I'm sat outside Green Park station; you wait for the same
Routemaster. We've never met before. You approach,
unprompted, and attempt to place a crumpled fiver in my hand.
You speak first; *Please take this, I want to treat you.* I'm not sure
of my role in this and there is no audience. I am on your nostrils.
Philanthropic urges have been unleashed. Who am I in this?
I am without direction. I pause, unsure of my lines, so I
improvise. *I don't need this, I work, I have money.* You look
at me; pity waterfalls off you and drowns the street we share.
Please, take it, you implore, *you're offending me.* I succumb,
reach out, and confirm the hierarchy between us.

WHEELCHAIR: LIGHTHOUSE OF THE STREETS

Everybody has a lighthouse.
Mine prowls angrily, barrel-chested,
on the headland.
It casts a light that pierces the great
salty blackness before it.

Stands like Poseidon.
Trident in one storm-worn
calloused hand,
a vast golden net in the other,
as though it will rest
only when the entire contents
of the ocean have been captured.

The green and yellow
lights of aurora
play like children above.
He's here, he's here,
my lighthouse bellows,
with a ferocity that fuels
the ocean and shakes
the foundations of Atlantis.

Vast cavernous vessels
turn into October gold leaves.
Move now or be wrecked
on the cliffs of my feet.
Washed away
and forgotten
like yesterday's footsteps
in the sand.

ONLY DESERT REMAINS

It's been twenty years since the end came. I have trekked across
the desert we once called somewhere else. This journey
has been made alone, across the arid sandy landscape.
Vegetation as sparse as the support I have shunned
in favour of stubbornness and a rucksack full of resolve.
I escaped Death Valley once. Then I was flanked by fellow
wanderers. Lost like me, searching for home. But then
I returned. And I faced this hostile horizon head-on. Without help.

Throughout this journey I've been hunted by packs of wild dogs.
They have expected me to fail, to fall, to give in and succumb
to their hunger. Chase me all you want. Follow my scent.
I have left it for you. But I will not give in. Ask yourself this.
By this point, having felt their hot breath and bared
teeth, would you know the end was near? If each night you'd
heard the desert jackal howl for more than half of your life
would you still be here, stronger than the day you set out?

Do not look at me and underestimate my strength.
As long as there is a beat in my chest,
do not tell me I am not able.
I am still alive.
I am still alive.
I am still alive.

STARTING AGAIN

I sit by classmates not seen in months. Turn the paper over, like they do. Critique my pre-accident English text, like they do. Ken – the central character – wishes to die. He is paralysed like I am now. I have nothing to write about Ken.

30,000FT

Escape artist:
a knife, bloody with strawberry and butter,
lies lifeless in the sink;
crumbs leave evidence that this hurried exit
had not gone to plan.
The duvet flung and left unmade. Radiators will bleed
for a week. Tracks not yet removed by January rays.
Manic, passport control, something to declare,
but not today. The Boeing and my airborne alibis
pierce through camouflage clouds. Too high to
cast a shadow.

Below, shaded eyes catch blinking lights. An SOS.
I call for anywhere but there.

THE BARBADOS WAVE

You, fearful of the ocean because your feet
won't touch the bottom.
Torn, because you want to help me fulfil a twenty-year dream.
Me, not wanting to ask for help.
Fearless of the deep blue because I can't feel a thing.
Us, searching for solutions on our first holiday away.

I sit in silence. Bittersweet citrus rolls around my mouth
and softens the sandpaper dryness. Hundreds of lemonade
bubbles abseil down my oesophagus. They land in formation
and build a dam to stop words I can't bring myself to speak.

Ahead of me the beach is a war, a match for what rages between
my ears. Every inch of shade a new territory to stake a claim.
A battalion of red colour swatches armourless with only their skin
left to remove. Prone soldiers scattered on sunlounger stretchers,
melted ice cream, warm beer.

My mission is not here on shore. I'm here to tame the ocean,
but wheels weren't built for sand. This soldier, too proud to ask
for help, especially here on our first posting away from home.
So you, my ever-patient comrade, begin to drag me across the
trenches on a paddleboard.

One by one sunburnt soldiers valiantly rise as last rations
of strength return. Over the men stride, red muscles flexed, eager
to impress their partners and mine. Ravenous hands grab
at the rope; each pull sends me further into my helpless shell.

When board hits water I'm pushed out like a paper boat.
Invigorated. Strong and upright I paddle until in the distance
the watching infantry become nothing more than the dust
of the fallen. My chest grows proud like a sail in the wind,
feet overboard like rudders, head amongst the clouds.

I'm not here to float; I'm here to swim. I sway once to the left, then, like a graceless submarine, fall to the right. With salt on my lips lost memories sail back from my childhood. I've not done this since the accident. The cold waters of Britain's beaches return to me. Saltwater tears lost in the ocean.

Back on the board, inches from dry land. The beach, once a battlefield, now a victory parade. *We did it*, I shout. We haven't. A Barbados wave slaps the cockiness out of me and I'm buried like a landmine.

I will not climb into my shell, I will not be dragged back to my wheels. I demand to be carried aloft.

FINDING MYSELF IN NYC

I put on a grey suit, white shirt and red tie.
Drink a vodka martini in a sugar-rimmed glass.
The authentic Madison Avenue experience.
Head towards a skyscraper sunset.
Each revolving door
spins out a hurricane of grand ideas.
With every roll along the sidewalk
I feel more like me.
Like me.
More. Me.

THE GREAT WALL OF CHINA

Thirteen thousand miles of ancient brick
twist and turn through mountains and deserts
like a ceremonial Chinese dragon.
All that history, and I get the spot
with a KFC, Burger King and
an accessible ramp.

Once atop the fearsome adversary I sit
on my throne like an imperial emperor.
This super structure was intended for feet,
not wheels. Yet here I am.
Proud and dignified with the Wall tamed.
Continents away from distant memories
of my early life in a chair trying to conquer
pavements and kerbs.

The search for serenity is shattered.
I realise I share this intimate moment
with what appears to be a billion other people.
All with their digital zoom lenses
pointing my way.

A coachload of happy tourists give me
the same strongman gesture
universally understood
irrespective of whether your tongue strokes
Mandarin or English.

I muse
why me here
is an even greater wonder
than that which
weaves beneath us.

BEFORE TIME

Dad was sixteen when he lost both parents.
The same age I was when I lost my legs.

I sometimes wonder
what he would have been like
had he not become an adult
while still a child.

The youngest of five
yet head of a family of one,
as each sibling came to terms
with their own grief.

I was twenty-one when Dad died.
I wish I'd had the chance to know him now.
As an actual adult.

Instead of a boy
caught up in his own trauma,
playing at grown-ups.

FIRST KISS

The first kiss. Leanne. We shrug off school rucksacks,
square up to each other like a playground fight.
Teenage tongues. Skip the bus home and jog
back through the clouds.

The first kiss. Caroline. This time someone leans down
to touch my lips. A sixth-form conga gallops past us,
red curls fall between my fingers, and I start
to remember normal.

The first kiss. You. The second time I've said *I do*.
I may now kiss my bride. Side by side, promises just made,
now and forever. Bound by a ring. The buds on your daisy-chain
crown bloom white. We embrace; a yellow sunrise is revealed.

TELL ME WHAT YOU KNOW THROUGH TAROT

PAST: THE NINE OF CUPS
Aged eight: build something, foundations till grave.
You want to follow Father. Twelve: shorthand to truth. Knock
on doors, two sugars, question. Sixteen: combustion control,
feline branches. The hero. You searched a life beyond
postcodes and peers.

PRESENT: THE KING OF SWORDS
Now you climb ladders without rungs. Bravery without flames.
Create space to be chair from chair. Play a symphony
on your skills. The earth is grid lines and structure.
You list. Pack. Sustain. Keep brawn on speed dial.
Build through agendas. I know who you are.

FUTURE: THE FIVE OF SWORDS
Sympathy card played. Separation on prescription.
Gold lines the inside. Chair still in hold. Wrinkled legs
won't make ninety. Right angles. Wrong perspectives.
You see working roots. Look straight with dignity. Never up.
Eight. Twelve. Sixteen. Did you expect more than this?

SETBACKS

*There is an egg-shaped sack of despair on my hip after I fall,
fully clothed, into an empty bath, then into a dark depression.
I'm confined to three weeks of bedridden solitary.*

THE THREE STAGES OF AGING

1.
Aged eight. Dad sits across from me.
He's brought a quarter of red sarsaparilla sweets
in a brown paper bag from Blackburn market.
I'm in a child's dressing gown in a grown man's
hospital ward. The white patch bandaged across
my eye hides the first opening scars, soon to be joined by
other thick worm-pink lines. These will come to tell the story
of me through a biography of accidents.

2.
Aged sixteen. I can tell Dad is nervous. His jokes
feel strained and his cough is thicker.
The metronomic beep of my heart monitor
breaks the heavy air of the intensive care unit.
It announces I've made another day.
He holds fear like a climber trying to carry Everest,
as he sits with sadness. I fight to keep this chapter open.

3.
Aged twenty-one. I watch Dad sleep. Hours earlier the doctor
advised me to go home and prepare
for the worst. Cancer has strangled his lungs.
I have learned nothing from the visits he made
and I want to ask what I am supposed to say.
But no more words will be spoken between us.
In the morning his book will close
and only my memories will make future pages of mine.

CLIMBING THE LADDER

Maggie sits opposite me, red plastic school chair to red plastic school chair, and asks what I'm good at. *Talking*, I say. *Talking*, she repeats, slower than me and with what sounds like a snide question mark rather than a full stop. She takes my shrug as an affirmation. With deliberate strokes she types that single word into a computer the size of the vast canyon of awkwardness that hangs between us.

Do you like people, being social, active and on your feet, and unpredictable hours? she says. *Yes, yes, yes, yes and I suppose so*, I offer back with a teenager's tetchy tongue. A Lothario of words still not evident in my refusal to speak. These in-depth answers feed the keyboard. Each tap jolts the silence that sits like the last guest at a party when all you want is bed and to ignore the exhausted dishes.

It is 12.22 and I've given up my lunch break to be here because I am hungry for careers advice, not the cheese and salad cream bread platters ignored in my rucksack.

I could be, should be, out on the netless tennis courts pretending I can play football with my mates. Or at a push a satellite on the very outer edges of Baz's orbit. Studying as he circles the girls with their knee-high socks and sideways giddy glances, whilst I take notes on how to be popular. But I know this isn't my forever. Next summer I'll leave with some certificates and a few letters from the alphabet that read like a Shakespeare rhyming scheme. I want the past five years of school to have counted.

So here I am, two minutes past my sandwiches. In a room under a stairwell in the prefab math block that smells too strongly of the boys' toilets next door. I know what I want to be; what I want is advice on how to be it. I tell Maggie I want to be a fireman, I think they are brave and I want to be useful.

She spots my inhaler, the same blue inhaler every boy in my school seems to carry so they have an excuse for not committing fully in the annual long-distance inter-year-group run. *You can't be a fireman if you have asthma*, she says. *Too much smoke and heroic exercise. It's not all cats lost in trees, you know. Let's do this questionnaire instead and see what else we can find for you.*

That's that, then. No fires and Mr November in charity calendars. If she was to ask I'd also offer that at various points in my life, which admittedly to this point has only been fifteen years long, I've wanted to be a builder, photographer, teacher, and country park ranger. A policeman, journalist, anything to do with Blackburn Rovers FC and even at one point our local MP. All of these are true. I know I don't want to sit behind a desk, my progress marked by the label on my suit upgrading with every job and pay-rise.

But she doesn't ask. Instead, I get a set of stock questions that just about drown out the sounds of those who'd had the right idea doing any activity other than this. Still, I am intrigued by what Maggie and her deskbound accomplice have in store for me.

Here we go, she says, reaching for the single sheet of paper as it labours out of the printer. Methodically she takes one glance and hands it to me with the expression of a newsreader telling the nation about the start of a nuclear war. I take the paper and look at two words. They bark their amusement at me in capital letters.

BEAUTY TECHNICIAN.

Now I am truly lost for words. This is a fine career choice, but this is not what I want to be or the advice I am after. I fold the paper, place it in the biro-stained pocket of my blazer where it looks like I've been shot with despair and then bled blue ink. I leave the room, without guidance, and walk towards the homing beacon of my friends.

What I don't know is that three months from now the accident I'm yet to have will render this conversation pointless. For the rest of my life ladders will forever be my nemesis and the next blue lights I see will be from the back of an ambulance, not the inside of a fire engine. There will, though, be a phone-book-length list of names that starts with Maggie of people I will spend my days trying to prove wrong. And twenty years later the boy on the red plastic school chair will become a man in a wheelchair and forever talk poetry.

UNDER APPEAL

Almost nonchalantly, in size 11 Times New Roman,
the letter states I have to attend an appeal hearing.
I am seventeen, eighteen months paralysed. I made the mistake
of branding stubbornness on my benefits application.
Stating I can dress, shave and make a cup of tea. Apparently
this classed as independence. So now I have to plead my case.
My solicitor tells me to be less obstinate, when I go face-to-face
with the clerk. I need to think of the times I need help. He says,
Don't be so proud; you will need assistance for life. I realise
my wheelchair will only leave me when I sleep in the ground. A
birthday ago I was deep in GCSEs and last days at school.
Today I'm taught a new lesson. To trade dignity for financial support
is the cost of disability.

THIS IS HOW IT FEELS TO BE...

Denied access to a flight because I didn't bring a carer
Ignored on dating websites when I post a photo that shows my chair
Segregated from fans I share a team with when watching the football
Asked if I need pushing when I haven't asked for your help
Bashful and embarrassed when asked if I can still have sex
Left on the train when pre-booked assistance doesn't arrive
Expected to ring a bell to request a ramp just so I can buy coffee
Determined to prove my worth

THE RACE

I'm 4,000 kilometres from home, pushing down the Lanzarote
promenade in my pimped-up low rider.
It's a high-tech, high-end, high-spec set of wheels.
Polished silver aluminium, handcrafted, made to measure.
Jungle-frog green aerodynamic wheels that wouldn't look
out of place in the Tour de France.
You could buy a new car and still have change for
a potpourri Magic Tree for the price of my machine.
This is some serious ride.

Four kilometres of smooth tarmac in front of me, six at the rear.
I'm in amongst the skaters, surfers, sun seekers and luminescent
Lycra-clad pushchair joggers. Playing chicken
with a family of five crammed into one of those bikes with Mum
and Dad up front and three on a bench at the back baffled
as to where the hell they plug their handheld in.
Dogs taking their owners for a walk.
I've got the sun on my face, the ocean whispering
love songs in my ear and all is good with the world.

Until he cycles past. You know the guy.
Out with the missus but always has his front wheel
just ahead of hers.
Grey polo shirt, beige cargo shorts, black socks
with that familiar white ticked swoosh and Puma trainers.
His holiday shop starts and ends at JD Sports. Doesn't write
a list of things to pack; just scoops the shit up
off the floor of his man cave and throws it in his
Engerland Engerland Engerland rucksack.
Seat too low, knees too high, Prince of the Promenade
or so he thinks.

As he sways past me like the swell of the ocean,
he looks over his shoulder and shouts, *Go on, son, I'll race you.*
I nod, give a half-there smile, raise a hand and do that
non-movement taxi hail kinda wave.
This is my stock response.

My learned behaviour.
Developed over the past two decades to regular gems of wisdom
like this; *that looks hard; have you got a licence for that; you'll
get done for speeding; watch out, mate, you almost ran me over.*

But what I really want to do is shout,
YOU'RE ON, LET'S DO THIS.
Just what does he expect to happen?
There's already a serious flaw with what he's said,
given he made the challenge whilst overtaking me.
What is he going to do? Stop,
give me a ten-metre head start.
He's on a fucking bike and he's using his legs.
You know, those luxurious legs that are propelling
him forward. Does he think there's actually a race?
A race implies some sort of competition.
Which, he's already established, as I watch his arse
wobble into the distance, does not exist here.

Here's the question. What is it he actually wants to say?
Well done on being out. Kudos for pushing myself,
for having the audacity to just carry on.
For not booking a one-way ticket to Dignitas.
He may mean well.
This might be ill-judged holiday banter
fuelled by a Guinness too many.

Guess what? I mean well too
when I give him the answer to his question
as I make a silent wave, turn my palm around
and tuck in my thumb and two smallest fingers,
and flick the V for victory.

*

Rewind twenty years. I'm in hospital.
Forty miles from home.
A scared sixteen-year-old
who has just eviscerated his spine.
I now have a cross stitched into my entire back,
and twelve inches of metal hold me together.
Spent two weeks on life support
and told I would never walk again.

I've got four more months of staring dead-eyed
at men weeping into their breakfast cereal
before being released back into a life
that suddenly looks very different.
I don't know if I'll get a job,
say *I do*, or hear the words
morning, Dad.
Learning to wash,
piss and get dressed again.
A grown-up man baby.

*

Fast-forward twenty years.
I no longer wake up to the stifled cries
of men trapped in unfamiliar beds,
in bodies they can't move
and lives they didn't ask for.

And no, I don't want a race,
because I've already won.

GARLIC BOY

The M&S ready meal you pick up
for a Friday night treat
with a bottle of sauvignon blanc
and a cheesecake for one.
That you put back on the shelf
because you can't stand
garlic.
Like the boy in a wheelchair
whose face you once kissed
and who treated you
with kindness.
That you put back on the shelf
just because he couldn't
stand.

WALKING AGAIN THROUGH AVATAR

Act 1
In 3D glasses I walk as Sully's blue-skinned
Na'vi, mobile again. I've got this. Folded
into my velvet cinema seat, somehow
unbalanced, running on feet not owned
for fifteen years. I breathe, I believe.

Act 2
Behind the glasses tears escape
the red-blue hue as I escape
into celluloid. Trapped by my
body, prisoner in the IMAX,
grateful for the black box darkness.

Credits
I'm not ready
to wrench atrophied legs from seat
to wheelchair. Groundbreaking. I ran.
The names of those who helped
me challenge surgeons' words
roll before my eyes.

GOING HOME

I do not want to leave. Here, I am normal.

UNWELCOME HOME

Summer is here. Suntans have long since replaced scarves.
At last, I'm home. I'd left half a year earlier on a snowy Saturday,

reluctantly wrapped in layers of wool. With an almost prophetic
warning, Mum had heated my ears about catching a death.

I am no longer in a coat, now a wheelchair. It's as I remember
and yet everything has changed. Almost like I've come through

the wrong front door. Set at my old height, even the mirrors
disdainfully snub my existence.

Mirror, mirror on the wall, why have I been ostracised
from the daily changing family portrait in the reflective glass?

Mum, brother, brother, only air where once were my eyes.
This was where I'd checked my school tie. The knot in my

stomach tightens with a loss I cannot yet articulate. It's not just
the mirrors that highlight the shame I can't see. The step

under the letterbox through which cold comfort condolence
cards are fed is adorned with an unwelcome mat just for me.

A dignity-eroding commode sits uncomfortably in the living
room. Everything out of reach but the kitchen sink.

What does it mean to call something a home? Whatever
this was, it no longer feels the way it once did. I am a stranger.

My family, rocked by tragedy, try to live as normal. While I –
ghost in the wheelchair – am unfamiliar in a once-familiar place.

ON THE NUMBER 76 IN BRISTOL

The disability spotter marks my arrival onto the bus
at Gloucester Road. She does so with the glee of a locomotive
enthusiast caressing the unchecked box in the pad saved
for the rarest of smoke breathers and tunnel divers. Eyes
collide. I am scanned as if in an airport X-ray
machine. In return, I behave as though there is a kilo
of white stuff lining the material that warms my nether
regions. Uncomfortably. I look anywhere but forwards. Focus
instead on the other passengers, who seem oblivious as we cut
through the kaleidoscope of Stokes Croft without a second
glance. A man with a crutch and crumpled duvet takes his seat
when we stop at the Bear Pit. I am forgotten. The double-decker
boundaries of inappropriate behaviour shift. The spotter's gaze
moves to a new interest.

SEEING ME AGAIN

I fantasise about what it would be
like to see a version of me stride down
Belgrave Road. Children in tow. The same table
tennis bats for hands, a standing six-foot-seven. Bastard.

Would we look away, as though old exes
who cannot let go? Or would I stare
and marvel at who he had become? Sun-
tanned, svelte, envy of the path.

I hope the other me would acknowledge
rather than ignore, would see the pride
I wear on these wheels, the confidence.
The man I have become.

LOVE IN AN IKEA BLUE BAG

I watch you water the plants
that sprawl like seventies flock wallpaper.
They were meant to be a futon,
but I returned from Ikea
with a car full of houseplants.
A declaration of wanting to grow.
You knew I would never water them.
I'd use the chair as reason not to.
Can't reach, I'd lie.
Decoration without responsibility.
You've cursed, re-potted,
put them in sunlight.
Our house
breathes
of you.

SCRATCHCARD MEMORIES OF DAD

I scrape fingernails at memories,
as if they were the flimsy silver layer
of an off-licence scratchcard. Desperate to reveal
moments that don't exist. Addicted,
I tell myself this will be the time,
this one will be a winner.

Of course, I do have photographs.
Boxes that overflow with childhood smiles,
a loft-full of dated hairstyles
and legs that work.
Ice creams in Southport, Christmas dinners
and paper hats; all now prisoners
in a cellophane cell.

Then came graduations, marathon finishes,
my two weddings with brides you never met.
Behind all the smiles and selfies,
there is a void where you should have been.

But, of course, you were never really absent.
In amongst the revelry and backslaps,
you were still there.
After the floral buttonholes have withered and dried.
I think of you. A forever sunset, your shadow cast
long into celebrations still to come.

WELLER'S WOOD

inspired by the song 'Wild Wood' by Paul Weller

Savage hawthorn presses aggressively
against bare brown birch trunks,
wrapped with scars and knots
like barbed wire and bad news.
Decay lurks everywhere.

Despite the desperation,
with no obvious way out,
this is a crossroads.
Give up or go on.
This wild wood
won't be forever.

Seasons change,
a vibrant bluebell carpet awaits.
Snowy bleak nightmares replaced
by white flowers of nightshade
and honeysuckle hearts.
Day by day green shades
of regrowth form in the canopy above,
like thick dense leaves of hope.

As I approach the outer edges,
the small solitary oak that led me here
is left behind with winter. What now?
This is not the way I came in.

Riches rain from above.
Life survives. In the way a captive
comes to rely on its kidnapper,
there was protection in the wood.
What breathes beyond this I do not know.

WHITE

Duplicitous white snow turns crimson beneath me.
A bloody outline seeping its way around my stricken frame.
Marking the dying body of the person I used to be.
An avalanche of activity in the time it takes a winter's
breath to form and disappear.
Through cries that climb
between barren brown branches
a single question thaws in my sixteen-year-old mind.

What happens next?

I rouse to the sound of sirens.
It is the last day of the Tour de France
and the gendarmerie are clearing the Champs-Élysées.
We are in Paris on our honeymoon.
You're facing me, and, for the second time in two days,
dressed in white again, only now wrapped in hotel sheets.
Confetti still in your hair, champagne still on your lips.
The corners of my mouth stretch for the grey at my temples.
Drunk on euphoria, I answer a twenty-year-old question.

We happen next.